My Mom is a Surrogate

by Abigail Glass, M.A.

illustrated by Riley Robertson

Victory Publications
victorybookpublishing.com
Printed in the United States of America

ISBN-13: 978-0-578-49534-7
ISBN-10: 0-578-49534-1

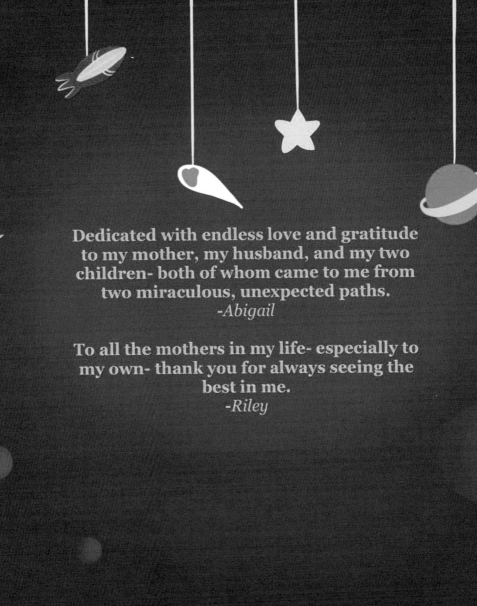

Dedicated with endless love and gratitude
to my mother, my husband, and my two
children- both of whom came to me from
two miraculous, unexpected paths.
-Abigail

To all the mothers in my life- especially to
my own- thank you for always seeing the
best in me.
-Riley

There are many different kinds

of families all around us.

Every person in every family grew inside someone's body, and then they were born!

There are many people who want to have a baby.

They hope, they wish and they dream they will become a mommy or a daddy.

Sometimes they hope for a long time.

Sometimes, they need help.

**Sometimes they need
someone else to grow and
carry the baby for them.**

**The lady who grows and
carries someone else's baby is
called a surrogate.**

A surrogate will get matched with the intended parent or parents, who are hoping to have a baby.

My mom is a surrogate.

She's carrying the baby for the intended parents.

Here are the intended parents of the baby
my mom will have.
They are the parents of the baby.

Draw a picture or place a photo of the intended parent or parents of the baby that your mom will have here:

My mom *is* going to be pregnant with the baby for a long time.

My mom's body will change; she will have a **big** pregnant baby belly.

My mom is giving an amazing gift: the gift of growing a baby for someone who can't. Even though she is pregnant and growing the baby, she won't be the mom of the baby when it is born. The baby will go home with its parents.

My mom will go to doctor
appointments to check on the baby.
My mom also talks to the intended
parents to let them know how she
and the baby are doing.

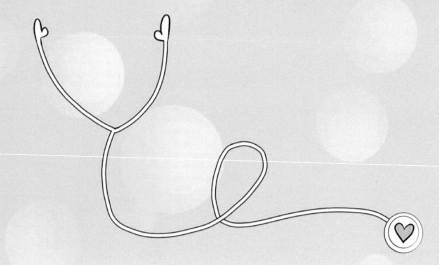

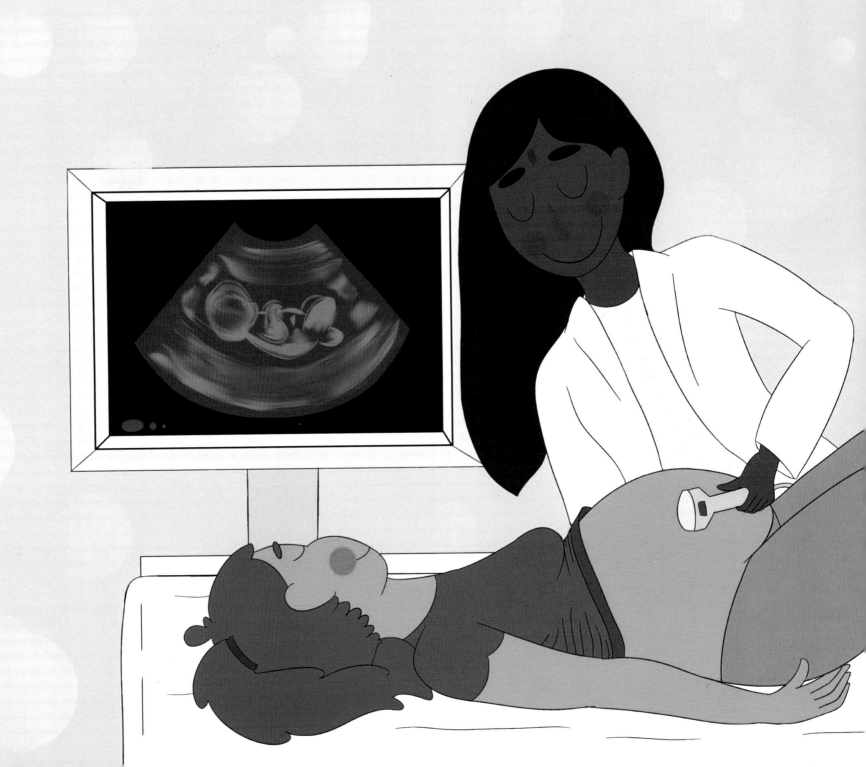

Sometimes, when I'm out with my mom, people will ask me if I'm going to have a baby brother or sister.

When the baby is ready to be born and come into the world, my mom will go to a hospital. The doctors and nurses will help her give birth to the baby.

I might get to meet the baby
or hold the baby while my mom is
at the hospital. Then, the baby will
go home with their mom or dad,
and my mom will come home to me.

Draw a picture or place a photo of the baby that your mom gave birth to here:

When I think about my mom being a surrogate, and about the baby, I can always look at a picture or drawing of the baby that my mom grew for another family.

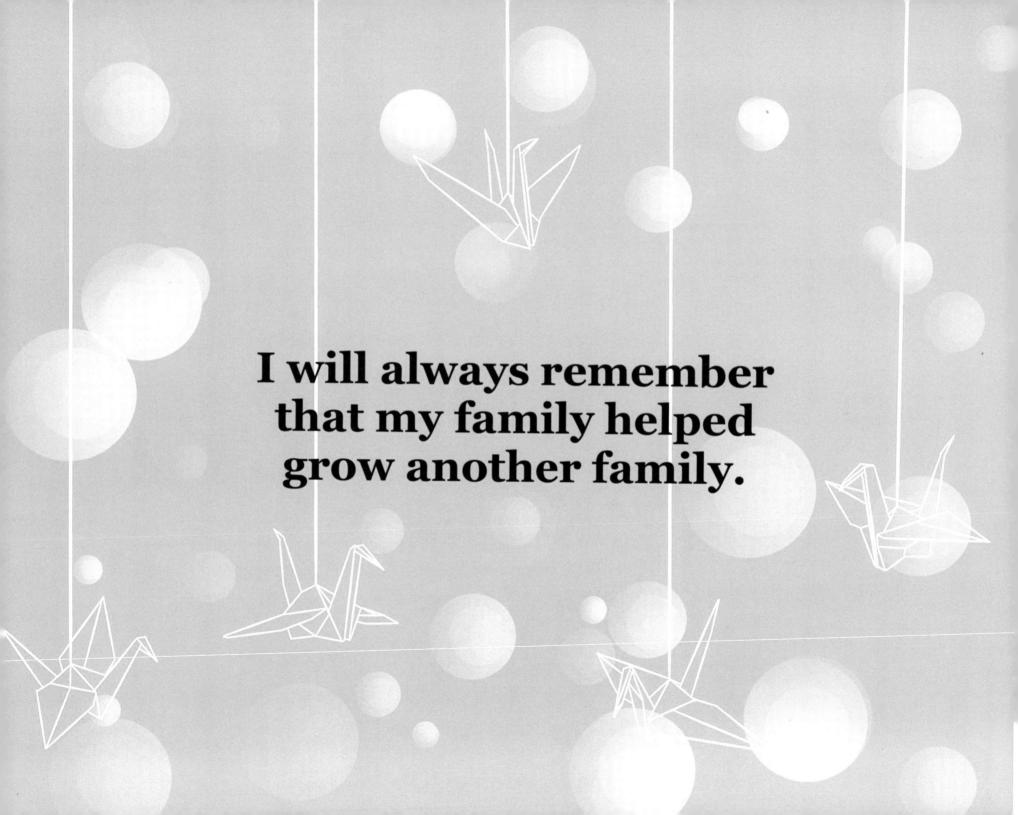

I will always remember
that my family helped
grow another family.

Abigail Glass is a psychotherapist in the Los Angeles area. She has been practicing for 18 years and has a specialty in all things related to growing families. Her own personal and professional experience with infertility, surrogacy and adoption have led her to a deep understanding and compassion for all those struggling to build their families.

Riley Robertson is a Los Angeles based artist who enjoys illustrating, painting, writing and photography. Riley has worked with families and children as a teacher and caregiver for more than a decade, and has developed lifelong relationships with both students and families in her community. She is an avid adventurist who loves traveling, scuba diving, hiking and experiencing new things.

Abigail and Riley met as neighbors and have forged a friendship that naturally unfolded into a combination of their talents leading to this book.

CPSIA information can be obtained
at www.ICGtesting.com
Printed in the USA
LVRC011730081119
636790LV00014B/340